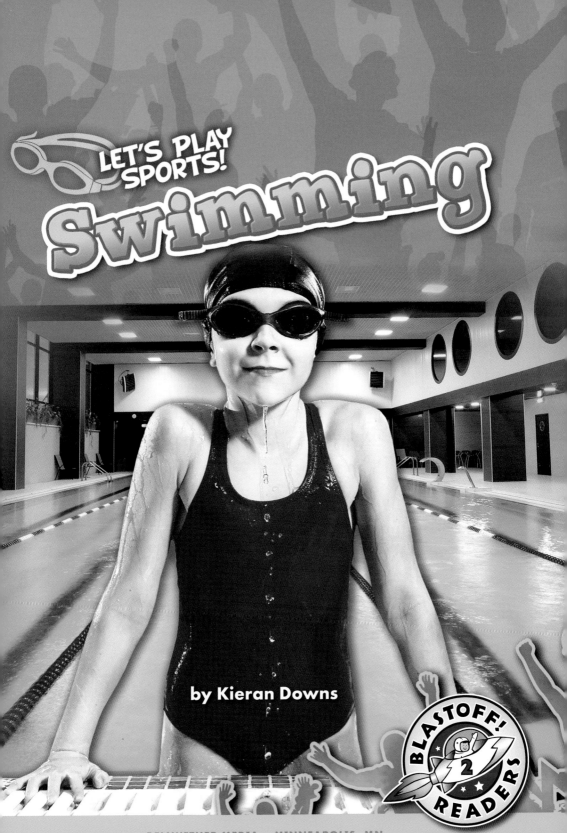

LET'S PLAY SPORTS!

Swimming

by Kieran Downs

BLASTOFF!
2
READERS

BELLWETHER MEDIA • MINNEAPOLIS, MN

Blastoff! Readers are carefully developed by literacy experts to build reading stamina and move students toward fluency by combining standards-based content with developmentally appropriate text.

Level 1 provides the most support through repetition of high-frequency words, light text, predictable sentence patterns, and strong visual support.

Level 2 offers early readers a bit more challenge through varied sentences, increased text load, and text-supportive special features.

Level 3 advances early-fluent readers toward fluency through increased text load, less reliance on photos, advancing concepts, longer sentences, and more complex special features.

★ **Blastoff! Universe**

Reading Level

Grade **K**

Grades **1–3**

Grade **4**

This edition first published in 2021 by Bellwether Media, Inc.

No part of this publication may be reproduced in whole or in part without written permission of the publisher. For information regarding permission, write to Bellwether Media, Inc., Attention: Permissions Department, 6012 Blue Circle Drive, Minnetonka, MN 55343.

Library of Congress Cataloging-in-Publication Data

Names: Downs, Kieran, author.
Title: Swimming / by Kieran Downs.
Description: Minneapolis, MN : Bellwether Media, Inc. [2021] | Series: Blastoff! readers: Let's play sports! | Includes bibliographical references and index. | Audience: Ages 5-8 | Audience: Grades K-1 | Summary: "Relevant images match informative text in this introduction to swimming. Intended for students in kindergarten through third grade"– Provided by publisher.
Identifiers: LCCN 2019053735 (print) | LCCN 2019053736 (ebook) | ISBN 9781644872178 (library binding) | ISBN 9781618919755 (ebook)
Subjects: LCSH: Swimming–Juvenile literature.
Classification: LCC GV837.6 D69 2021 (print) | LCC GV837.6 (ebook) | DDC 797.2/1–dc23
LC record available at https://lccn.loc.gov/2019053735
LC ebook record available at https://lccn.loc.gov/2019053736

Editor: Christina Leaf   Designer: Josh Brink

Printed in the United States of America, North Mankato, MN.

Table of Contents

What Is Swimming?   4

What Are the Rules for   8
   Swimming?

Swimming Gear   18

Glossary   22

To Learn More   23

Index   24

What Is Swimming?

Swimming is a sport in which people race in water. It often takes place in pools.

Swimmers race as individuals or on **relay** teams. The fastest time wins the race!

4   relay team

Swimming is popular around the world. Swim events are called meets.

swim meet

MICHAEL PHELPS

- Team USA
- Individual and relay events
- Accomplishments:
  - 23 Olympic gold medals
  - Most medals at a single Olympic Games
  - Most Olympic medals of all time

Most people watch the sport during the **Olympics**.

What Are the Rules for Swimming?

freestyle

There are four **strokes** used in swim races. Freestyle is the fastest stroke. It is also called the front crawl.

Swimmers swim the
backstroke on their backs.

backstroke

Swimmers kick their legs like a frog for the breaststroke. For butterfly, swimmers kick their feet like a dolphin.

breaststroke

butterfly

Swimmers do every stroke in **medley** races.

Swimmers start races on **blocks**. The swimmers get ready when the **starter** tells them to take their marks.

They **dive** into the water on the starter's **signal**.

block

dive

The pool is broken up into **lanes**. Each swimmer gets their own lane.

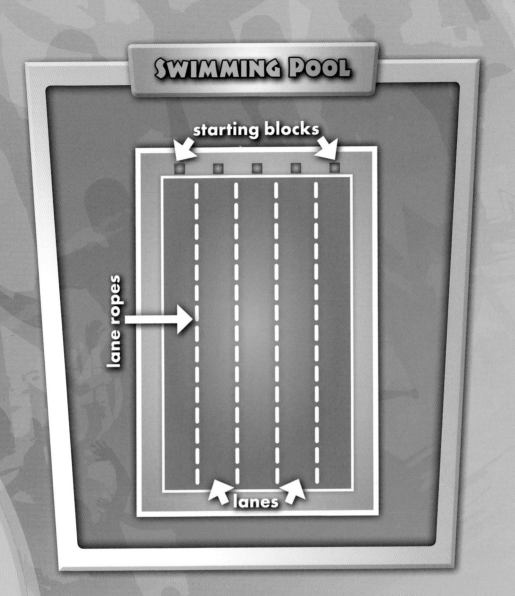

SWIMMING POOL

starting blocks

lane ropes

lanes

Swimmers on the same relay team share a lane.

Olympic pools are 164 feet
(50 meters) long. Each race
is a certain distance.

Whoever touches the wall
in the fastest time wins!

Swimming Gear

Swimmers wear tight swimsuits that lessen **drag**. This helps swimmers go faster.

SWIMMING GEAR

swim cap

goggles

swimsuit

Swim caps also cut down on drag.

Goggles protect eyes
and let swimmers
see underwater.

Take your mark
and dive in!

goggles

Glossary

blocks—raised platforms that swimmers dive off of to start a race

dive—to jump headfirst into water

drag—a force that slows down an object; drag causes a swimmer to go slower.

lanes—long parts of a pool marked by lines

medley—a race that includes every kind of stroke

Olympics—short for the Olympic Games; the Olympic Games are worldwide summer or winter sports contests held in a different country every four years.

relay—related to a race in which multiple people work as a team; in swimming, relay teams usually have four members.

signal—a motion, action, or sound that is used to give an instruction

starter—the person in charge of starting a swim race

strokes—the different ways of swimming

To Learn More

AT THE LIBRARY

Lajiness, Katie. *Katie Ledecky: Olympic Swimmer.* Minneapolis, Minn.: Abdo Publishing, 2017.

Morey, Allan. *Swimming and Diving.* Mankato, Minn.: Amicus High Interest, 2016.

Rebman, Nick. *Swimming.* Lake Elmo, Minn.: Focus Readers, 2019.

ON THE WEB

FACTSURFER

Factsurfer.com gives you a safe, fun way to find more information.

1. Go to www.factsurfer.com.

2. Enter "swimming" into the search box and click $\mathcal{Q}$.

3. Select your book cover to see a list of related content.

Index

backstroke, 9

blocks, 12

breaststroke, 10

butterfly, 10, 11

distance, 16

dive, 12, 13, 20

drag, 18, 19

freestyle, 8

gear, 19

goggles, 20

individuals, 4

lanes, 14, 15

medley races, 11

meets, 6

Olympics, 7, 16

Phelps, Michael, 7

pools, 4, 14, 15, 16

race, 4, 8, 11, 12, 16

relay teams, 4, 15

starter, 12

strokes, 8, 11

swim caps, 19

swimsuits, 18

time, 4, 17

water, 4, 12, 20